Meg and Greg

Frank and the Skunk

Frank and the Skunk

with

nk ng tch dge

Four Phonics Stories

Written by
Elspeth Rae and Rowena Rae

Illustrated by
Elisa Gutiérrez

ORCA BOOK PUBLISHERS

Published in Canada and the United States in 2020 by Orca Book Publishers.
orcabook.com

Library and Archives Canada Cataloguing in Publication
Title: Frank and the skunk : with four phonics stories / written by Elspeth Rae and Rowena Rae ;
illustrated by Elisa Gutiérrez.
Names: Rae, Elspeth, 1973- author. | Rae, Rowena, author. | Gutiérrez, Elisa, 1972- illustrator.
Description: Series statement: Meg and Greg | Orca two-read ;
2 Identifiers: Canadiana (print) 2020018962X | Canadiana (ebook) 20200189638 |
ISBN 9781459824935 (softcover) | ISBN 9781459824942 (PDF) | ISBN 9781459824959 (EPUB)
Subjects: LCSH: Reading—Phonetic method—Problems, exercises, etc. |
LCSH: Reading—Phonetic method— Study and teaching (Elementary) |
LCGFT: Instructional and educational works.
Classification: LCC PS8635.A39 F73 2020 | DDC jC813/.6—dc23

Library of Congress Control Number: 2020930593

Summary: This partially illustrated workbook, meant to be read by an advanced reader with a
beginner reader or struggling reader, combines stories and exercises that focus on phonics.

Orca Book Publishers is committed to reducing the consumption of
nonrenewable resources in the production of our books. We make
every effort to use materials that support a sustainable future.

Orca Book Publishers gratefully acknowledges the support for its publishing programs provided
by the following agencies: the Government of Canada, the Canada Council for the Arts and the
Province of British Columbia through the BC Arts Council and the Book Publishing Tax Credit.

Design and illustration by Elisa Gutiérrez

Printed and bound in Canada.

26 25 24 23 • 3 4 5 6

*For all the children who have started to get to
know and love Meg and Greg.
—E.R. and R.R.*

*For my sister, Loli, with whom I have read many
stories and have enjoyed many adventures.
—E.G.*

In this book:

nk

ng

tch

dge

Contents

How to read
the stories in
this book

Meg and Greg is a series of decodable phonics storybooks for children ages 6 to 9 who are struggling to learn how to read because of **dyslexia** or another language-based learning difficulty. The stories are designed for a child and an experienced reader to share the reading, as shown in the diagram above. A child feeling overwhelmed at reading sentences could start by reading only the illustration labels. More about this approach is on page 153.

What is included in these stories

The stories in this book are for a child who is familiar with all the basic **consonant** sounds (including **consonant blends**), **short vowel** sounds and the four letter combinations (**phonograms**) introduced in *Meg and Greg* Book 1 (**ck**, **sh**, **ch**, **th**). The stories in this book introduce the following phonograms: **nk**, **ng**, **tch** and **dge**. Each story uses previously introduced phonograms, so by the final story, a child is practicing all four new phonograms.

The stories also use a few common words that can be tricky to sound out. These words are in the list to the right. The child you're reading with may need help with them. We recommend writing the words on a card that can double as a bookmark. If you're curious about what makes these common words tricky to read, flip to pages 150–151.

Warning!

These words look little, but they can be tricky to read.

a

as, has

is, his

of

the

do, to

I

be, he, me, she, we

OK

New for this book

have, give

you

"all" family
(ball, small, etc.)

9

This story
introduces **nk** as in *blink*
and *sank*. The letter combination
(**phonogram**) **nk** is the only way
in English to spell the /nk/ sound.
The phonogram **nk** makes a
single sound that is very different
from the individual sounds of
the letters *n* and *k*. Try making
the sounds /n/, /k/ and /nk/, and
notice how the position of your
tongue differs for each one. It's
quite difficult to pronounce /nk/
without a preceding vowel. Try **ank**,
ink, **onk**, **unk** (*bank*, *sink*, *honk*,
bunk). English doesn't have words
ending with **enk**.

This story focuses on words
with the sound /nk/ spelled with
nk. It also includes the four
phonograms introduced in *Meg
and Greg* Book 1 (**ck**, **sh**, **ch**, **th**).
For a list of **nk** words,
including all the ones
used in this story, go to
megandgregbooks.com.

Frank
and the
Skunk

A story featuring

Frank

stink

skunk

Chapter 1

The **Prank**

Meg and Greg stood in line to get their cabin numbers at Camp Nut-Hatch.

"I'm so excited that we get to stay at camp for two weeks this year!" Meg said.

Greg nodded. "Me too. One week is way too short."

At last Meg and Greg reached the front of the line. The camp leader, named **Hank**, was checking everyone in.

"Hi Meg. Welcome back! You're in cabin four, the Mad **Mink**."

Meg whooped. "Yes! That's the best cabin!"

Next **Hank** turned to Greg. "Hi Greg. Great to see you again this summer. You're in cabin nine, the Chill **Chipmunk**."

Hank

Greg got his backpack.

Let's get to the cabins, Meg.

Will you get a top **bunk**, if you can?

Yes, I **think** I will. Will you?

You bet!

CABINS
1 – 8
9 – 16

Meg walked into the Mad **Mink** cabin. Two other girls were sitting on the top **bunks**.

"Hi, I'm Meg."

"I'm Jasmin," one girl said.

The other girl was fiddling with some plastic toys on her pillow. She looked up. "I'm Emma."

"You can have the last top **bunk**, if you want," Jasmin said.

"Awesome." Meg **plunked** her backpack onto the **bunk** bed.

Emma flashed a grin at Meg.

Mad **Mink** cabin

bunk bed

Jasmin

Emma

Do you do **pranks**, Meg?

Yup!

We have a plan to do a **prank**.

OK. And the plan is . . . ?

To stick this stuff in **Hank's** cabin.

frog

bugs

Meg got up on Emma's **bunk** bed.

That will give him a shock! Let's do it.

Jasmin, Emma and Meg walked up the path.

"Which is **Hank's** cabin?" Meg asked.

Emma grinned. "I asked him at check-in. He's in the Big Bobcat cabin."

chipmunk

They found **Hank's** cabin. Jasmin crept up to a window and peered through. "I **think** it's OK. I can't see anyone."

Emma tiptoed up the cabin steps, clutching the toy bugs, frogs and snakes. She slipped inside, and Jasmin followed. Meg stayed outside to keep a lookout.

Thunk!

Ack! A dog!

I **think** that's **Frank!**

Frank

Meg, stop that dog!

Frank!

Frank!

Frank!

A small dog ran past Meg.

Chapter 2

Frank on the Run

Frank

Meg, Emma and Jasmin ran down the path after **Frank**.

Meg looked into the trees. "Which way did he go?"

"That way." Jasmin pointed.

"Let's stop for a second and listen," Meg said.

The three girls stood still.

Suddenly a twig snapped.

"I **think** I hear him!" Jasmin said.

Greg saw the dog's pointy tail disappearing behind a tree **trunk**. "There he is!"

Meg ran toward the dog, and the others followed.

Frank darted left and right. He ran around trees and under bushes.

trunk

Frank

"**Frank**, stop!"

"**Frank**, come here!"

"Yip! Yip!"

Chapter 3

Frank Stinks of Skunk

Frank whimpered. He **slunk** away from the bushes.

"Poor **Frank**!" Meg said. "You scared a **skunk** and got sprayed."

The dog lay on his belly, whining.

"My eyes are watering," Jasmin said.

"I can't stand that smell! It's **rank**!" Emma wailed. "I **think** I'm going to puke."

"I know what to do about **skunk** smell!" Jasmin said. "We need to wash **Frank** in tomato juice."

Greg shook his head. "I tried that once with my dog, Rocket. It didn't work. But then we used baking soda and dish soap. That did the trick!"

Jasmin nodded.

I can get that stuff at the mess hall.

stink

trunk

Let me help you. I can't stand the smell.

Thanks! Meg and I can get **Frank** to a **sink**.

The dock has a big **sink** to gut fish.

OK. We will be as quick as we can!

Frank

Greg rubbed **Frank's** ears. "You **stink, Frank**! Meg, I need something to pick him up with."

"How about your T-shirt?" Meg asked.

Greg cringed. "No way!"

Meg laughed. "OK, fine. I guess I can get a towel from my cabin."

Meg fetched a towel, and Greg wrapped **Frank** in it. "Let's go and give you a bath!"

When Meg and Greg got to the dock, Jasmin and Emma were already there with a big box of baking soda and a full bottle of dish soap.

Greg filled the **sink** on the dock with water. He mixed in lots of baking soda and soap.

OK, Meg. **Plunk Frank** in the **sink!**

Frank

sink

He can't fit!

That's OK. I can still scrub him.

Jasmin, can you dust him with that stuff?

Sit still, **Frank!**

Frank whined, but he sat still. Greg rubbed baking soda into his fur.

Meg laughed. "Oh, **Frank**! You don't look like a brown sausage dog anymore. You're a bubbly, white mess!"

"I **think** it's working," Jasmin said.

Meg nodded. "Me too. I can't smell the **skunk** as much."

Emma took her hands off her face. She sniffed the air with a **wrinkled** nose. "Phew! He smells a bit better now!"

sink

dock

Next we have to get this **gunk** off **Frank's** back.

Dunk him in the **sink**.

But **Frank** can't fit in this **sink**.

We can **dunk** him off the end of the dock.

dock

Yes, that will do the trick!

Chapter 4

Dunk That Dog!

Meg wrapped **Frank** in the towel. The kids walked to the end of the dock. Meg knelt down on the wooden **planks** and **dunked Frank** in the water. Greg rubbed his hands through **Frank's** fur, and he scooped water onto the dog's head.

gunk

Frank wriggled. "Hold still, **Frank**!" Meg said. "Whoa, **Frank**, stop!"

Meg fell sideways and bumped into Jasmin.

Meg, Greg, Jasmin and **Frank** all fell off the dock.

Frank

Splash!

You OK?

Yes. Can you help me get **Frank** back up on the dock?

Yip! Yip!

That got all the **gunk** off him!

yank

Meg, Greg and Jasmin climbed up the wooden **planks** on the dock's ladder.

A lifeguard sprinted along the beach toward the kids. "You kids OK?" she called.

"We're fine!" Greg called back, hiding **Frank** in the towel.

Meg, Greg and Jasmin stood dripping on the dock. "Yes, just testing the water."

The lifeguard frowned. "You kids shouldn't be down here. Lunch is in five minutes, and then there's a welcome meeting by the flagpole."

"Right. **Thanks**." The four kids headed for the path.

"That was close," Greg whispered.

Chapter 5

The **Prank** Ends with a **Wink**

Greg and Meg dashed up the path toward **Hank's** cabin. Greg kept **Frank** wrapped in the towel.

"Hi kids!" **Hank** trotted up behind them on the path. "It's time to go for lunch. Can I give you a hand?"

Meg **blinked**. Greg's heart **sank**.

Hank

skunk

Frank

Hank's cabin

Emma and Jasmin arrived at the cabin just as Greg was **yanking** the door closed.

Greg grinned. "We did it! **Frank** is back where he belongs."

The three girls and Greg all high-fived each other.

"**Thanks** for helping us with **Frank**, Greg," Meg said.

Greg smiled. "No problem. But next time you girls do a **prank**, I'm staying out of it!"

Hank's cabin

BIG BOBCAT

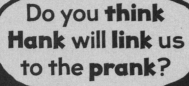

trunk

Hank

After lunch all the campers sat in a circle by the flagpole.

Hank stood up. "Welcome to Camp Nut-Hatch! I'd like to start by introducing you all to our camp dog. His name is **Frank**, and he's very friendly."

Hank paused and glanced in the direction of Greg and the Mad **Mink** girls. Then he kept speaking. "Earlier today **Frank** was treated to a nice bath, **thanks** to some friends."

Blink, blink!

The four kids looked at each other.

"Are we in trouble?" Emma whispered.

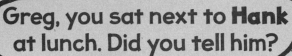

Greg, you sat next to **Hank** at lunch. Did you tell him?

Sh . . .

Greg! You let it slip?

I did *not!*

Was **Frank** still wet as you let him in **Hank's** cabin?

Yes, I **think** his back was wet.

Then **Hank** must have felt **Frank's** back.

That must be it.

Hank smiled. "The friends also left a nice gift for our craft table."

"What is it?" someone asked.

"Frogs, bugs and snakes. Fake ones, of course."

"Oh no!" Emma muttered. "Now we really are in trouble."

Hank turned slowly toward the Mad Mink girls and Greg.

The kids held their breath, but Hank just smiled and gave them a wink!

wink

A bunch of the camp kids went to pet **Frank**, but the dog ran past them.

Hank

Frank

I got a dog kiss!

Give me a kiss, **Frank**.

That's just dog smell, Emma.

wag

Not me! He still smells of **skunk**!

The End

Turn the page for more practice with **nk** words!

nk
spelling

Spell each **nk** word below the picture.
One letter fits into each box.

nk

nk
match-up

Draw a line from each *nk* word to the correct picture.

sink

trunk

stink

skunk

drink

bunk bed

wink

nk
word wheel

How many words can you think of using the letters from the wheel? Start every word with a letter or a letter combination from the outer ring. Then use a vowel from the middle ring. End the word with **nk**.

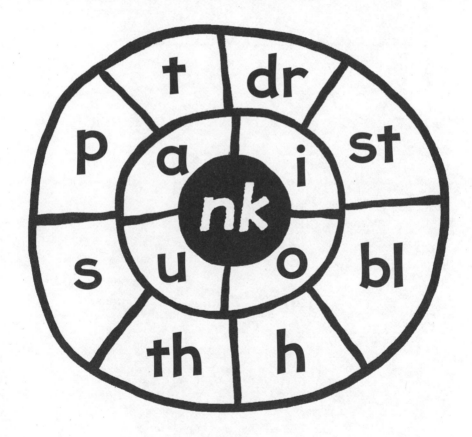

This story introduces **ng** as in *swing* and *bang*. The letter combination (**phonogram**) **ng** is the only way in English to spell the /ng/ sound.

The phonogram **ng** makes a single sound that is very different from the individual sounds of the letters *n* and *g*. Try making the sounds /n/, /g/ and /ng/, and notice how the position of your tongue differs for each one. It's quite difficult to pronounce /ng/ without a preceding vowel. Try **ang**, **eng**, **ing**, **ong**, **ung** (*sang*, *strength*, *wing*, *strong*, *lung*).

The very common suffix -ing is pronounced in the same way, but suffixes have not yet been introduced in the *Meg and Greg* books, so words with this suffix are not included in the kid's text.

This story focuses on words with the sound /ng/ spelled with **ng**. It also includes **nk** words for continued practice, as well as the four phonograms introduced in *Meg and Greg* Book 1 (**ck**, **sh**, **ch**, **th**).

For a list of **ng** words, including all the ones used in this story, go to megandgregbooks.com.

The
King's Long
Fangs

A story featuring

Chapter 1

Sing a Song of Bing Bong

Meg and Greg sat together at breakfast. Hank, the camp leader, stood and **rang** a bell to get the campers' attention.

"Good morning, campers! Today I have a fun challenge for you. First, get yourselves into groups of two."

Meg and Greg glanced at each other.

Hank continued. "Each group needs to make up a skit. And here's the fun part: you have to use as many words as you can that end with the letters **ng**. For example, in the words **bang**, **bing**, **bong** and **bung**."

Meg clapped. Greg groaned.

Hank grinned. "You have until lunchtime, and I have a prize for the best skit. Good luck!"

"Where should we go to work on our skit?" Meg asked.

Greg shrugged. "I don't care."

Meg bumped her friend's shoulder. "Come on, Greg!"

Greg made a face. "I wish we could do a **Ping-Pong** challenge instead. *That* would be fun!"

Meg laughed. "Tough luck, Greg! Let's go to the **swings**. I always get good ideas when I'm on a **swing**."

Meg skipped across the field, **singing** at the top of her **lungs**. Greg trailed behind her.

song

swings

Chapter 2

The **King** of **Bling**

Meg **flung** herself onto a **swing**. Soon she was **swinging** as high as the treetops.

Greg watched Meg for a minute and then sat on the other **swing**.

swing

"How about I make up the story?" Meg called. "And you write it down? Then we can practice acting it out together."

"I guess I can write it down," Greg said. "But I'm not acting in it. You can do that."

Meg grinned. "Well, let's start with the story. We need paper."

Greg started writing.

swing

"And he uses his **fangs** to **ring** a **gong** . . ."
Meg continued.

"Wait," Greg said. "I can't write that fast.
He's the **king** of where?"

grass

Bling.

Got it. The **king** of **Bling** has **long fangs.**

Yes, and the **king bangs** a **gong** with his **fangs.**

king

long fangs

gong

A **gong** . . . ?

"A **gong**?" Meg gave Greg a surprised look. "It's a big metal disc that **hangs** sideways. It makes a booming sound when you **bang** it . . ."

gong

Greg interrupted. "I know *what* a **gong** is. I just think it's weird. Where is this story going, Meg?"

Meg shrugged. "It's weird . . ."

swing

...but it's got lots of **bang**, **bing**, **bong** in it.

trunk

OK, OK!

The **king** **bangs** the **gong** with his **fangs**...

Got it.

Next?

Chapter 3

Spring and the Mustang

Meg **swung** back and forth for a few minutes. "I know!" she said. "The **king rings** the **gong** to play music for a girl called ... **Prong**."

"**Prong**? What kind of name is that?" Greg asked.

"Fine. What about **Clang**? A girl could be named **Clang**."

Greg laughed. "No way! That's even worse."

"Well, can you think of a name that ends with *ng*?" Meg asked.

"Let's use **Spring**," Greg said. "I go to school with a girl called **Spring**."

Meg gave Greg another surprised look. "A **mustang** is a wild horse."

"Oh. I thought you meant a **Mustang** car," Greg said.

"Well, I guess **Spring** could have a car or a horse," Meg said, "but I like the idea of a wild horse in the land of **Bling**."

"What does this have to do with the **king ringing** the **gong** with his **long, strong fangs**?" Greg asked.

gong

This time Meg laughed. "I don't know! I'm just using every **ng** word I can think of!"

Greg laughed too.

Meg continued the story. "So **Spring** rides her **mustang** all the time. One day the **king** wants to go with her."

Greg looked at Meg. "**Hang** on. Let's give the **king** his own **mustang** horse to ride."

"But he doesn't know how to ride a horse," Meg said. "And he wants to be friends with **Spring**."

Greg **flung** his pen on the ground. "You're not going to turn this into a love story, are you?"

Meg grimaced. "No!"

Greg blew out his breath. "Phew. That's good. We have to act this out in front of everyone!"

Meg grinned and clapped her hands.

"Hooray! You said 'we.' That means you are going to act in the skit after all!"

"Well, I guess I will . . . " Greg said.

Chapter 4

The **Fang** Dentist

Greg sat and waited.

Meg **swung** back and forth, thinking. "Let's see." She closed her eyes.

swing up

swing back

"I know! The **king** goes to a dentist to get the **fangs** taken out."

"Great idea!" Meg said. "Her name can be **Tang**, and she's really good at taking out **long fangs**."

Greg twirled his pen. "Who's going to play the dentist in the skit?"

"I can play **Spring** *and* the dentist," Meg said. "So . . ." She thought some more. "How should Dentist **Tang** pull out the **fangs**?"

Tongs!

She can tug on the **fangs** with **tongs**.

Yes! But the **king** has to be held still.

Dentist Tang

OK...

Tang asks a **gang** of **strong** kids to help.

gang of strong kids

The kids grab the **king** and **hang** on. Then **Tang** can tug.

Tang tugs!

fangs

tongs

Twang!

Meg grinned at Greg. "This will be such an awesome skit, Greg!"

"I guess so. But can we end it now?" Greg asked.

Meg shook her head. "The **king** smiles at **Spring** and says, 'No more **fangs**! Now will you take me for a ride on your **mustang**?'"

Greg wrote on the pad.

"And then," Meg continued, "**Spring** says, 'Yes! I always wanted to be your friend, but your **long fangs** were so scary!'"

Chapter 5

The King's Long Fangs

After lunch Hank asked who wanted to be first to perform their skit. Meg **sprang** to her feet. "We will!"

box of props

Greg put his arms over his head, but he got up and followed Meg.

"Does your skit have a title?" Hank asked.

Meg grinned. "Yes. *The King's Long Fangs*."

"Sounds great! The stage is yours," Hank said, sitting down on a bench.

All the campers laughed and clapped. One of them stood up to **fling something** onto the stage. "Here! Use these vampire **fangs**, Greg!"

fangs

Greg picked up the plastic **fangs** and put them in his mouth. He grinned, and all the campers clapped even louder.

king of Bling

The End

Turn the page for more practice with **ng** words!

ng
rhyming

Think of a word to rhyme with:

bang　　**gang**　　_____

ring　　**swing**　　_____

strong　　**long**　　_____

lung　　**stung**　　_____

ng
word search

Find the following words in the puzzle.
Words are hidden ➜ and ↓.

b d h h a n g t v r r u

a q z s t r i n g s p z

n e p u n k x e g w o h

k d x f a n g d a i z o

s t r o n g z k n n o t

x p s p r i n g g v t

m g u l u n g p i n k p

x u n h o n k h b m u j

		Bonus words:
fang	spring	bank
gang	string	honk
hang	strong	pink
lung	swing	punk

ng
sorting *ng* and *g* words

Spell each word in the correct list, **ng** or **g**.

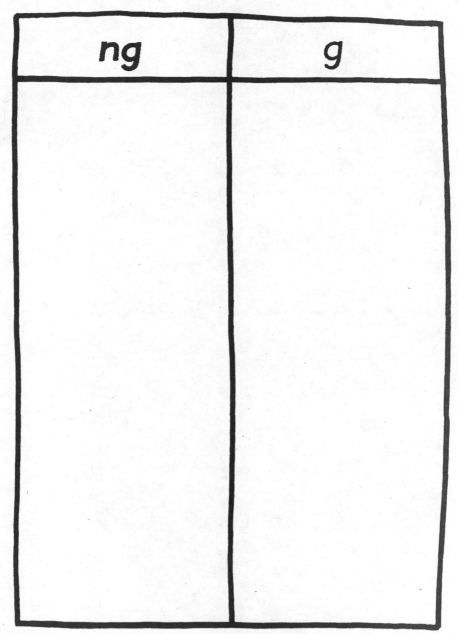

ng	g

This story introduces **tch** as in *clutch* and *stitch*. The letter combination (**phonogram**) **tch** is one way in English to spell the sound /ch/. Other ways are **ch** (*chin*, *lunch*) and **tu** when these letters appear side by side in words with a Latin suffix (*temperature*, *moisture*). The **ch** spelling was introduced in *Meg and Greg* Book 1, so it appears in this story. The **tu** spelling is not included in the kid's text.

The main thing to know about **tch** is that it only ever comes immediately after a short vowel, as in the words *fĕtch* and *cătch*. The phonogram **tch** appears at the end of a syllable and most frequently in one-syllable words. There are a few exceptions where the sound /ch/ is not spelled **tch** after a short vowel, like *much*, *such* and *sandwich*. We have not used exceptions in the kid's text.

This story focuses on words with the sound /ch/ spelled with **tch**. It also includes **nk** and **ng** words for continued practice, as well as the four phonograms introduced in *Meg and Greg* Book 1 (**ck**, **sh**, **ch**, **th**).

For a list of **tch** words, including all the ones used in this story, go to megandgregbooks.com.

The Catch That Went Bad

A story featuring

tch

Mitch

catch

Dutch Dash

Chapter 1

A **Glitch** in the Trip

Meg blinked her eyes and **stretched** her arms. They hurt from three days of paddling a canoe, but she didn't care. She loved canoe camping, and **Mitch**, the trip leader, always made the adventure so fun.

She glanced over at Jasmin and Emma. They were both still asleep with their sleeping bags pulled up to their noses. Meg wriggled out of her own sleeping bag and unzipped the tent.

Just as she poked her head into the morning sunshine, she heard the sound of someone **retching** and then throwing up!

tent

Meg frowned. "The crab? The one you and Jack went out to **catch** yesterday morning?"

Mitch nodded, **clutching** his stomach.

"It made you sick?" Greg asked.

"It must have gone bad," **Mitch** said. "Or maybe I didn't cook it enough."

"Who else ate the crab last night?" Meg asked.

"Just Jack and me," **Mitch** said.

"Now what do we do?" Greg asked.

crab

Jack

After **Mitch** and Jack went back to bed, Meg **stretched** out on the grass next to Greg's log. "I guess we need to wait here while they rest."

Greg **scratched** a mosquito bite on his leg. "This is a bit of a **glitch**. We're supposed to canoe to Anvil Island and camp there tonight."

"I hope **Mitch** and Jack will be well enough to paddle later," Meg said.

"We could skip staying on Anvil Island and paddle right back to Camp Nut-**Hatch**," Greg said.

"It's too far to paddle in one day," Meg replied. "Especially if **Mitch** and Jack feel sick."

Greg nodded. "Good thing our canoe trip is almost over."

The **Dutch** Dash Tips

Mitch and Jack appeared around lunchtime.

"How are you two feeling?" Emma asked.

Jack shrugged. "A bit better."

Mitch nodded. "I think we should get going."

"The canoes are already packed," Greg said.

"Great work, kids! Jack and I might be paddling the **Dutch** Dash a bit slower than usual today," **Mitch** said.

"It's OK, **Mitch**," Meg said. "We have **hitched** your canoe to ours, so we can tow you and Jack."

Mitch smiled. "Thanks."

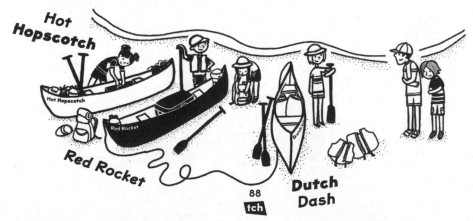

Hot Hopscotch

Hot Hopscotch

Red Rocket

Red Rocket

Dutch Dash

The kids held the **Dutch** Dash still. **Mitch** and Jack got in.

All set?

Yup!

Yup!

Hang on . . .

. . . is that Jack's hat on the log?

Yes, I think it is.

patch

hat

log

I can **fetch** it.

Greg and Jasmin paddled a canoe called the *Hot **Hopscotch***, and Meg and Emma were in the *Red Rocket*. **Mitch** sat at the back of the ***Dutch** Dash* with Jack at the front.

"Everything all right back there?" Greg called over his shoulder.

When Greg didn't hear anything, he twisted around in his seat. **Mitch** and Jack were both leaning over one side of their canoe.

Dutch
Dash

"**Switch** sides, **Mitch**!" Greg yelled. "You guys are going to tip!"

"Too late," Jasmin said.

Chapter 3

The **Dutch** Dash Melts

Jasmin hopped out of her canoe. She helped Jack and **Mitch** onto shore, while Greg pulled the canoes up the rocky beach.

"That water is cold!" Jack said.

"Sit in this **patch** of sun," Jasmin said. "I'll find some dry clothes for you."

Meg carried the **kitchen** box ashore. She began setting up the camp stove on the overturned canoe.

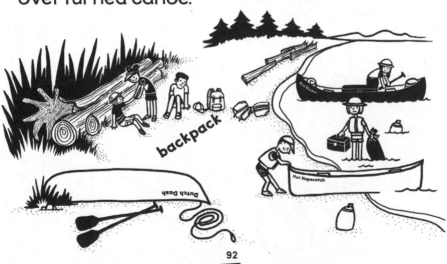

backpack

Dutch Dash

Soon Jack and **Mitch** were in dry clothes and sipping a hot drink.

"What a day!" Meg said. "Let's hope we don't have any more **glitches**."

"My mom says things always happen in threes," Jasmin said.

Emma laughed. "Don't jinx us, Jasmin!"

"Uh-oh," Greg exclaimed. "I think we already have another **glitch**."

Meg looked at the spot where Greg was pointing. "Oh no! The stove burned the canoe?"

Chapter 4

To Anvil to **Pitch** the Tents

Meg hung her head. "I can't believe I burned a hole in the **Dutch** *Dash*!"

Jasmin inspected the hole. "Can we **patch** it?"

"We don't have anything to **patch** it with," Greg said. "Let's stash the canoe behind those big rocks. Someone can **fetch** it later."

"How will we get six people back to Camp Nut-**Hatch** with two canoes?" Emma asked.

"Three people in each canoe," Meg said.

Jasmin nodded. "We'll just have to leave some things behind."

Greg and Emma got the **Dutch Dash** up to the big rocks.

We can fit this bag in the *Red Rocket*.

And we can fit the **kitchen** box in the *Hot **Hopscotch***.

Greg, can we stash the rest of the stuff with the **Dutch** Dash?

Yup. It all fits.

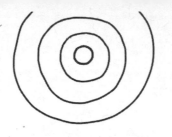

The paddle to Anvil Island took all afternoon.
Mitch and Jack slept on and off during the trip.

When they got to the island, Greg, Meg,
Jasmin and Emma hopped out and pulled
the canoes up the beach. **Mitch** and Jack
crawled out.

"The campsite is up the hill," **Mitch** said.

"Let's go and check it out," Greg said. "We
can come back to **fetch** the tents."

Jack **clutched** his tummy. "I don't feel good."

"You and I can wait here, Jack. I'm still not
feeling great either," **Mitch** said.

logs

The kids ran up the track to the top of the hill.

sunset

The sun will set in a bit. We have to **pitch** the tents.

Let's **pitch** them on this soft **patch** of grass!

OK. I can **fetch** the tents.

The kids could hear the dinner bell ringing at Camp Nut-**Hatch** across the water.

Emma rubbed her stomach. "I'm hungry after all that paddling!"

"Me too," Greg said. "Let's get dinner started as soon as we finish **pitching** the tents."

Meg glanced down the trail. "What is taking Jasmin so long?"

scratch

patch of grass

Chapter 5

The **Thatch** Hut

Emma groaned. "Now what do we do?"

Jasmin gazed across the water. "Should we paddle back to Camp Nut-**Hatch** tonight?"

Greg shook his head. "No, it will be dark before we get even halfway across."

"We have to build some kind of shelter," Meg said.

Jasmin nodded. "We can stack driftwood and sticks against something and then sleep underneath."

Meg clapped. "Perfect! Instead of **pitching** a tent, we're building a **thatch** hut!"

Emma scanned the clearing. "But where can we build it?"

Jasmin **fetched Mitch** and Jack and explained what they had done. When **Mitch** saw the hut, he grinned for the first time all day. "You kids deserve a medal for this!"

Mitch and Jack unrolled their sleeping bags in the **thatch** hut and went straight to sleep.

thatch
hut

Meg and Jasmin got a fire started, while Greg and Emma carried the **kitchen** box up from the beach.

Do we still have hot dogs left?

kitchen box

Let me check in the **kitchen** box.

Yup. We have lots of hot dogs, buns and **ketchup**.

And let's mix up a **batch** of muffins!

This is the best . . .

In the morning **Mitch** and Jack woke up early.

"How do you feel, Jack?" **Mitch** whispered.

Jack grinned. "Hungry!"

"Me too. Let's make breakfast."

Jack and **Mitch** carefully climbed out of the **thatch** hut without waking the others. Jack whisked up eggs and grilled ham. **Mitch** made hot chocolate and a fresh **batch** of muffins.

"Breakfast is ready!" **Mitch** called.

Mitch

Jack

Let's pack up and get back to Camp Nut-**Hatch**!

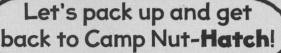

log

Hot Hopscotch

Red Rocket

Jump in, kids! But let's **switch** spots.

Me at the back of the *Hot Hopscotch*, and Jack at the back of the *Red Rocket*.

Red Rocket

Hot Hopscotch

Meg, Greg, Jasmin, Emma, you get to rest in this last **stretch**!

Thanks, **Mitch**!

Red Rocket

Hot Hopscotch

This is fun!

The End

Turn the page for more practice with **tch** words!

tch
word ladder

Climb down the ladder by solving the clues and changing just one letter from the previous *tch* word. You'll know you've done it right if the word at the bottom of the ladder matches the one at the top.

Hatch

1. Hatch

2. When you bake muffins or cookies, you make a _____ of them.

3. If someone throws you a ball, you try to _____ it.

4. The thing that holds a gate or door closed.

5. A pirate often has one of these over one eye.

6. To throw the ball to the batter in a baseball game.

7. A lady dressed in black and riding on a broomstick.

8. A narrow trench dug along the sides of roads for water to run into.

9. A person from the Netherlands (Holland) is _____ .

10. The cage for a small animal like a rabbit to live in.

11. When baby birds break out of their eggshells.

tch
match-up

Draw a line from each *tch* word to the correct picture.

witch

patch

stitch

scratch

match

switch

crutch

Also available at megandgregbooks.com

tch
sorting *tch* and *ch* words

Spell each word in the correct list, **tch** or *ch*.

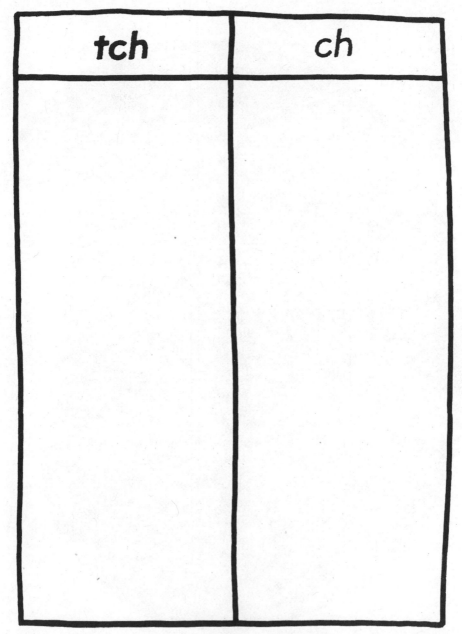

tch	ch

This story introduces *dge* as in *lodge* and *badge*.

The letter combination (**phonogram**) *dge* is one way in English to spell the sound /j/. Other ways are **j** (*jump, jam*) and soft **g** when it is followed by the vowels *e*, *i* or *y* (*general, ginger, gym*). Since the **j** spelling is a basic consonant, it appears in this story. The soft **g** spelling is not included in the kid's text.

The main thing to know about *dge* is that it only ever comes immediately after a short vowel, as in the words *hĕdge* and *brĭdge*. The phonogram *dge* appears at the end of a syllable and most frequently in one-syllable words.

This story focuses on words with the sound /j/ spelled with *dge*. It also includes *nk*, *ng* and *tch* words for continued practice, as well as the four phonograms introduced in *Meg and Greg* Book 1 (*ck*, *sh*, *ch*, *th*).

For a list of *dge* words, including all the ones used in this story, go to megandgregbooks.com.

Fudge!

A story featuring

Chapter 1

Madge Is the Best!

Greg stretched out on the grass. "I can't believe tomorrow is the last day of camp."

Meg nodded. "I know! It's sad, but the last day is always fun with the boat regatta and ceremony."

"What's a *regatta?*" Jack asked.

"Boat races. They're lots of fun," Greg said. "And after the races, there are prizes."

"It's also when they give out **badges** for cleanest cabin and stuff like that," Meg said.

"I hope the **judges** give us a **badge** for best-decorated cabin," Jasmin said.

Just then **Madge** the cook came up to the four kids.

Greg licked his fingers. "Great idea! Let's make her a **badge** for being the best camp cook ever."

badge

"I have an even better idea!" Meg said. "Let's decorate her kitchen too."

Jasmin clapped her hands. "Yes! We can sneak in and do it tonight, so she gets a surprise in the morning."

"I'm in!" Jack said. "Where's the kitchen?"

Meg giggled. "Right there, Jack. At the back of the **lodge**."

"Greg? Are you in?" Jasmin asked.

Greg frowned. "Sneak out after lights-out?"

"Come on, Greg. It's for **Madge**," Meg said.

"OK. I guess so. I'll come too."

At dusk, the kids met on the small **bridge** that led to the **lodge**.

bridge

All set?

Yup. We have the **badge**.

And we have all this stuff to hang up in **Madge's** kitchen.

OK. Let's get to the **lodge**!

badge

MADGE is #1

Sh . . . !

hedge

The kids crept along, staying in the shadow of a **hedge**. When they got to the **lodge**, Greg and Jack crept up the front steps and peered through the dark window.

"Check the door," Meg said. "Maybe it's unlocked."

"Nope," Jack called out. "It won't **budge**."

Greg **nudged** Jack. "Sh . . . you'll wake someone up!"

Jasmin snuck around to the back of the **lodge**.

One by one, the four kids squeezed through the gap and jumped from the window **ledge** to the floor. They crept down the hallway and through the **lodge** toward the kitchen.

"It's pitch black in this **lodge**. I can't see a thing!" Meg said.

"Me neither," Jack said.

Frank

"Sh!" Greg said. "I think I hear something."

Meg stopped suddenly to listen.

Bam! The others slammed into her. One, two, three!

Chapter 2

A **Smudge** of **Fudge**

Greg crawled toward Jack. "**Fudge**? Let me have some."

Meg groaned. "Are you two serious? We've just destroyed this cake! **Madge** probably spent all day making it, and all you can think about is stuffing it in your mouths!"

Greg giggled.

Jack licked his fingers. "Why was this big cake left out here in the middle of the **lodge**?"

"It must be for celebrating the last day of camp tomorrow," Jasmin said.

Greg squinted at the ruined cake. "Meg, lift up your hand. There's writing on it."

Camp Nut-Hutch R...?

The last bit is a big **smudge**.

smudge

A big **smudge** of **fudge**. Yum!

Let me have a lick.

Greg! Jack!

Stop it.

fudge

Meg got up off the floor. "Let's be serious for a minute. We have to fix this cake."

Jasmin nodded. She got up too. She and Meg each grabbed an **edge** of the table and lifted it back onto its feet.

Meg knelt back down and started **nudging** bits of the cake back together. "This is gross." She lifted the cake pan and slid it onto the table.

Jasmin gazed at the smashed cake. "It's totally wrecked. The words are all **smudged**, and a whole piece is missing. We can't leave it like this!"

"Sure we can," Greg said, still licking his fingers. "Just smooth it over."

We can't. It's in bits.

It's a big **splodge** . . .

. . . of **fudge.**

Ha! Ha! Ha!

CAMP NUT-HATCH REGATTA!

We have to fix this mess.

splodge

And fast. It's past ten!

OK. Let's get in **Madge's** kitchen.

KITCH

Jack frowned. "Why do we need to get in the kitchen?"

"To bake a new cake!" Meg said. "And we'll have to clean up this mess too."

Greg's eyes lit up. "Jack, you and I can 'clean up' this mess of yummy **fudge**!"

"You guys sure love that **fudge**!" Jasmin said. "Don't take too long. We'll need help in the kitchen."

Jasmin led the way. "I'll look for **Madge's** recipe book."

"Great," Meg said. "I'll start getting eggs and things out of the **fridge**."

fridge

Chapter 3

Fudge Muffins

Meg and Jasmin peered at the muffins.

"Are they **fudge**?" Jasmin asked.

"I can't tell. Let's taste one," Meg said.

Meg took a muffin and broke it in half. She gave one piece to Jasmin.

"Yum! They *are* **fudge** muffins!" Jasmin said.

"Perfect," Meg said. "We can line them up and cover them in frosting. They'll look like one big cake."

"But what will **Madge** say when she can't find her muffins?" Jasmin asked.

"Well," Meg said, frowning, "let's worry about that later. For now let's just make frosting to cover the muffins."

Jasmin shrugged. "OK. But we need butter to make frosting."

Greg unlocked the **fridge** and opened it. "What do we need to bake a new cake?"

"We don't need to bake a new one," Meg said. She explained the plan to use the **fudge** muffins.

"Great idea! Then what do we need to make frosting?" Greg was still looking into the **fridge**.

"Just butter from the **fridge**," Jasmin said.

"Why don't we use this?" Greg asked. He held up a tub marked **Fudge** Frosting.

Meg clapped her hands. "Perfect!"

Chapter 4

Fudge Butt

Frank

"This looks awesome! No one will know anything happened," Jack said.

"Except **Madge**," Meg said, "but let's worry about one thing at a time."

Jasmin nodded. "We need to get this new cake onto the table in the **lodge**."

Greg carefully slid the cake pan off the **edge** of the counter. Jack held the kitchen door open for him.

"Yip! Yip!"

Greg jumped. "Yikes! Frank!"

Jack laughed. "That was close. The cake nearly fell on the floor all over again!"

Yip!

Crash!

Splat!

Splodge!

Frank?

The dog sat in the kitchen, stuck in the tub of **fudge**.

Frank!

fridge

mop

badge

Jack looked into the kitchen and laughed again. "Oh, Frank! What have you done?"

Greg poked his head through the doorway.

"Your butt is covered in **fudge**, you rascal!" Greg said.

Jasmin wrinkled her nose. "I guess we can't put that tub of frosting back in the **fridge** now!"

A clock in the **lodge** chimed eleven.

Meg gasped. "It's getting late! We haven't even decorated the kitchen yet!"

Meg got the tub of **fudge** off Frank.

Greg gave Frank a quick scrub.

Jack got a mop.

Jasmin strung up lots of ribbons. Meg hung the **badge** on the **fridge**.

MADGE is #1

The kids left Frank on his bed in the **lodge** and crept back to the cabins.

Chapter 5

Camp Nut-Hatch Rocks!

The next morning **Madge** headed into the kitchen early. "Wow!" she exclaimed. As she admired the decorations, she heard a knock at the door. She turned to see Meg, Greg, Jasmin and Jack. **Madge** smiled. "Did you kids do all this and make the **badge** on the **fridge** too?"

"Um, yes," Greg said. "But we need to apologize to you."

Meg explained what had happened, and the four kids showed **Madge** the new cake.

"Thanks for being honest, kids," **Madge** said. "*Camp Nut-Hatch Rocks!* is better than *Camp Nut-Hatch Regatta!* But there's just one problem left. Those muffins were for this morning's snack break . . . "

Later that morning the Camp Nut-Hatch Regatta began. Everyone lined the water's **edge** to watch each race. In the first race, Meg and Jasmin tipped their sailboat and had to be towed back to shore. They warmed up while eating **fudge** muffins and cheering on Greg and Jack's dragon-boat team.

Afterward the campers all gathered in the **lodge**. Hank, the camp leader, gave ribbons to the regatta winners. Then it was time to award the Camp Nut-Hatch **badges**.

"The **judge** had a hard job this year!" Hank said. "You have been a wonderful group of campers."

After all the excitement over the **badges**
had died down, Hank cleared his throat.
"Thank you for two great weeks!" he said.
"Now it's time for **Madge's** cake!"

Madge stood by the kitchen door, smiling.

"What a cool cake!" Hank exclaimed. He
bent over to read the top of it. "*Camp
Nut-Hatch Rocks*! It sure does!"

The End

Turn the page for more practice with **dge** words!

dge
word mix-up

Find the incorrect **dge** word in these speech bubbles.

A big batch of muffins sat on a ridge next to the sink.

Meg went to the bridge.

Jasmin, will it help to smidge this stick in the gap?

The dog sat in the kitchen, stuck in the tub of sludge.

Thanks, kids! This hedge is the best!

The kids met at the sledge.

Also available at megandgregbooks.com

dge
crossword

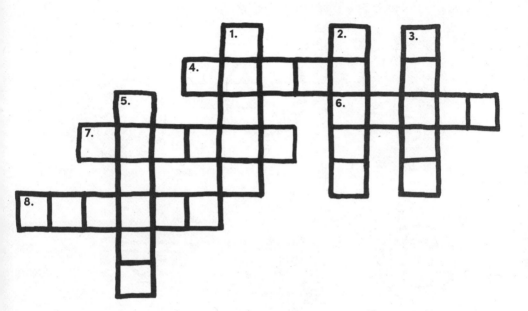

Across ➡

4. A sweet treat made with sugar, butter and milk.
6. In the game of _____ ball, you try to hit people on the other team with a ball but not get hit yourself.
7. You put milk in the _____ to keep it cold.
8. A word that means "a tiny little bit of something."

Down ⬇

1. Someone who hears cases in a law court and decides if an accused person is guilty or innocent.
2. A kind of fence made by planting bushes close together.
3. Something police officers use to prove their identity.
5. People and cars use this to get from one side of a river to the other.

Also available at megandgregbooks.com

dge
sorting dge and j words

Spell each word in the correct list, **dge** or *j*.
Hint: one picture/word will go into both lists.

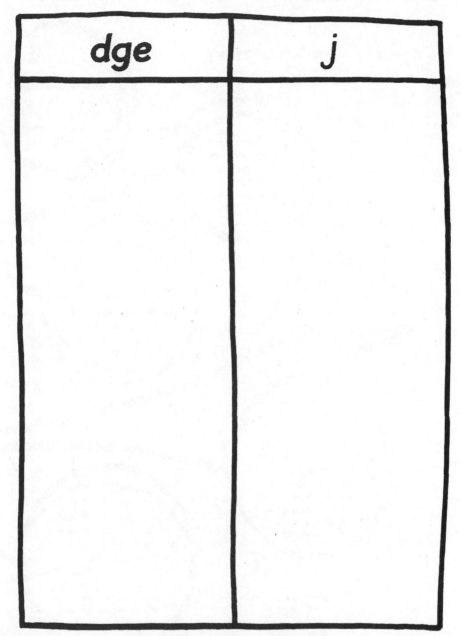

dge	j

149

dge

Some oddities of English explained

Do you know what's tricky about these little words?

This little word can be pronounced with a **short vowel sound** (/ă/ as in *hăt*), **long vowel sound** (/ay/) or **schwa vowel sound** (/uh/).

Children might try to pronounce this word as /off/ instead of the pronunciations /uv/ or /ov/.

Children might try to pronounce this word as /ock/ instead of reading the two individual letters.

Children might try to pronounce these words with short vowel sounds, as in /daw/ and /taw/, or even long vowel sounds, as in /doe/ and /toe/, instead of the pronunciations /doo/ and /too/.

Children might be confused by the letter *e* at the end of these two words. They might try to pronounce it, but it's a silent letter. Read more about the role of silent *e* in words ending with the sound /v/ on page 152.

This word is pronounced /y/–/oo/. It's fairly common for the letters *ou* to be pronounced with an /oo/ sound (*soup*, *group*), but it's unlikely that beginning readers will be aware of this sound for these letters, so they might need help reading it.

a
as, has
is, his
of
the
do, to
I
be, he, me, she, we
OK
have, give
you
"all" family (ball, small, etc.)

If these words followed the standard English spelling convention, they would all end in a double s, as in *pass* and *kiss*. Instead, they have a single s and are pronounced with a /z/ sound.

This very common word starts with the *th* letter combination (**phonogram**) and ends with a schwa-sounding vowel. The *th* phonogram is the focus of the fourth story in *Meg and Greg* Book 1.

In these words, the vowel makes a long sound, which children reading this book may not be familiar with yet.

Words in the "all" family are pronounced /ŏ/-/l/. Beginning readers might try to pronounce the letter *a* as /ă/ as in *hăt* and so pronounce "all" as /ă/-/l/.

Do you know what's cool about the letter *v*?

In English a word never ends with the letter *v*, so the silent *e* must be added. As well as the two words used in the stories in this book (*give*, *have*), there are many examples: *curve*, *olive*, *nerve*, *solve*, *twelve*.

As well as "protecting" the letter *v* at the end of a word, the silent *e* has several other functions in English. Stay tuned for *Meg and Greg* Book 3 to learn more.

Do you know why some words have double consonants?

Early scribes, who were often monks, used double consonants for several reasons.

They doubled a consonant to indicate that the previous vowel makes a short sound (*rabbit*, *bottom*, *hill*, *boss*). Not all words got this treatment, but one group got the double consonant quite consistently. They are the Buzz Off Miss Pill words, which are all one-syllable words with a short vowel and ending in *z*, *f*, *s* or *l*. Some historians suggest that the scribes wanted to show how the sounds made with these four letters can be carried on for a few seconds, rather than stopping abruptly like they do with the letters *t*, *b*, *p* and others.

The scribes also doubled consonants at the end of many small words, either to make the word longer or to differentiate it from a similar-sounding word. In English, content words (nouns, most verbs, adverbs, adjectives) tend to be three letters or longer. One- and two-letter words tend to be grammatical function words (pronouns, articles, prepositions, conjunctions and a few others) such as *me*, *a*, *of*, *or*. Therefore the scribes sometimes added a consonant (or a silent *e*) to make a content word longer. Examples are *egg*, *odd* and *inn*. In the case of the word *butt* (used as a chapter title in the story *Fudge!* in this book), the extra *t* was likely added to differentiate the noun from the function word *but*.

About the
Meg and Greg stories

Who are the *Meg and Greg* stories for?

These stories are for children who are struggling to learn how to read because they have dyslexia or another language-based learning difficulty.

We wrote the stories especially for struggling readers who are ages 6 to 9 (approximately grades 2–4), which is a little older than most kids start learning to read. These slightly older learners can understand and appreciate more complex content, but they need it written at a lower reading level. You might see this concept described with the term *hi-lo*.

To make a hi-lo concept work for children at a near-beginner reading level, we designed the *Meg and Greg* stories for shared reading. A buddy reader—an adult or other confident reader—shares the reading with the child who is learning. Each story has five short chapters and is ideal for use in one-on-one or small-group reading sessions.

Aren't there already lots of books for beginning readers?

Yes, but the many leveled readers available for beginners typically don't meet the needs of children with a learning difficulty. These children benefit from learning English incrementally and without spelling exceptions or advanced spellings thrown into the mix.

The *Meg and Greg* stories introduce one letter combination (**phonogram**) at a time. Each story builds on the previous ones by including words with the phonograms already introduced.

How does shared reading work?

Each story has several layers of text so that an adult or buddy reads the part of the story with more complex words and sentences, and the child reads the part of the story with carefully selected words and shorter sentences.

Each story has:
- *Illustration labels* for a child just starting to read or feeling overwhelmed at reading sentences. The labels are single words or short phrases and contain the story's target letter combination (**phonogram**) as often as possible.

- *Kid's text* for a child who has mastered the sounds made by the **basic consonants** (including **consonant blends**), **short vowels** and the four phonograms introduced in *Meg and Greg* Book 1 (*ck, sh, ch, th*). The kid's text appears on the right-hand page when the book is open to a story. We also used kid's text for all story and chapter titles. As we created the stories, we bound ourselves to a set of rules that controlled the words we were "allowed" to use in the kid's text. If you're interested in these rules, they are listed on our website (megandgregbooks.com).

- *Adult or buddy reader's text* is the most difficult, and it always appears on the left-hand page when the book is open to a story. The buddy text uses longer sentences, a wider vocabulary and some phonograms and other language elements that the beginning reader has likely not yet learned, but it avoids very difficult words.

A child who is a more advanced reader and simply needs practice with the target phonogram can try reading all three layers of text in the story.

Are there any tips for buddy readers?

Yes! Try these ideas to help the child you're reading with:
- Keep the list of tricky words handy for the child to refer to when reading (see the list on page 151).
- Before starting to read a story, have the child read the story title and each chapter title (in the table of contents). Ask them to predict what the story might be about.
- Before starting a story, write down a list of all the words the child might not be familiar with and review them together.
- Before you read a page of buddy text, have the child point out all the words with the target letter combination (**phonogram**) on the left-hand page of the open book.
- After reading each chapter, have the child speak or write one sentence that uses some of the words from the chapter. Some children might like to draw a picture.

Do the stories use "dyslexia-friendly" features?

Yes. As well as the language features throughout the story, we used design features that some people find helpful for reading:
- The font mimics as closely as possible the shapes of hand-printed letters. Children begin by learning to print letters, so we think it is important for the letter shapes to be familiar. For example, a child learns to print *a* not a and *g* not g.
- The illustration labels are printed in lowercase letters as much as possible because children often learn to recognize and write the lowercase alphabet first. A beginning reader may be less familiar with the uppercase letter shapes.
- The spaces between lines of text and between certain letters are larger than you might see in other books.
- The kid's text is printed on shaded paper to reduce the contrast between text and paper.

Glossary

Consonant: Any letter in the alphabet except for the vowels (*a, e, i, o, u*). The term *basic consonant* refers loosely to the main pronunciation of each consonant. For example, a student who knows the basic consonants will be familiar with the main sound for the letter *c* (/k/ as in *cat*), but not the less frequent sound for the letter *c* (/s/ as in *city*).

Consonant blend: Two or three consonants appearing at the beginning or end of a syllable. Each consonant sound is pronounced, but the sounds are so close, they seem to be blended or "glued" together. For example, *flop, camp* and *sprint*.

dge: A letter combination (**phonogram**) introduced in this book. It is one way in English to spell the sound /j/. Other ways are *j* (*jam*) and soft *g* when followed by the vowels *e, i* or *y* (*danger, margin, gym*). The phonogram *dge* only ever comes immediately after a **short vowel**, as in the words *bădge, plĕdge, rĭdge, dŏdge* and *bŭdge*.

Dyslexia: A term made up of *dys*, meaning "difficult," and *lexis*, meaning "word." Dyslexia tends to be used as a catchall term that describes a range of language-learning difficulties. These can include reading (fluency and comprehension), spelling, writing, organization skills (executive function) and even some aspects of speech.

Long vowel sound: The way in English that a vowel sounds when we pronounce it for a long time (longer than for **short vowel sounds**) in regular speech. Long vowel sounds are often represented by a silent or magic *e*, a combination of vowels or a single vowel ocurring at the end of a syllable. For example, *bīke, mūte, rāin, trēe* and *gō*. The horizontal line, called a macron, shows that the vowel is pronounced with a long sound. (Compare with the entry for short vowel sound.)

ng: A letter combination (**phonogram**) introduced in this book. It is the only way in English to spell the sound /ng/. The phonogram *ng* makes a single sound that is very different from the individual sounds of the letters *n* and *g*. Try making the sounds /n/, /g/ and /ng/, and notice how the position of your tongue differs for each one. It's quite difficult to pronounce /ng/ without a preceding vowel. Try **ang**, **eng**, **ing**, **ong**, **ung** (*bang, length, sting, long, sung*).

nk: A letter combination (**phonogram**) introduced in this book. It is the only way in English to spell the sound /nk/. The phonogram **nk** makes a single sound that is very different from the individual sounds of the letters *n* and *k*. Try making the sounds /n/, /k/ and /nk/, and notice how the position of your tongue differs for each one. It's quite difficult to pronounce /nk/ without a preceding vowel. Try **ank**, **ink**, **onk**, **unk** (*sank, pink, honk, trunk*). English doesn't have words ending with **enk**.

Phonogram: Any letter or combination of letters that represents one sound. For example, the sound /k/ can be spelled with five different phonograms: **c** (*cat*), **k** (*kite*), **ck** (*stick*), **ch** (*echo*) and **que** (*antique*).

tch: A letter combination (**phonogram**) introduced in this book. It is one way in English to spell the sound /ch/. Other ways are **ch** (*chin*) and **tu** when these letters appear side by side in words with a Latin suffix (*temperature, moisture*). The phonogram **tch** only ever comes immediately after a **short vowel**, as in the words *bătch, skĕtch, dĭtch, nŏtch* and *crŭtch*.

Schwa vowel sound: The way in English that we often pronounce the vowel in an unstressed syllable, like the *a* in *yoga*. A vowel pronounced as a schwa sounds similar to /uh/. This is the most common vowel sound in the English language! Any vowel can be pronounced as a schwa: *a* in *balloon*, *e* in *forgotten*, *i* in *pencil*, *o* in *person* and *u* in *until*.

Short vowel sound: The way in English that a vowel sounds when we pronounce it for a short time in regular speech. For example, *ăt, nĕt, pĭg, tŏp* and *ŭp*. The doohickey, called a breve, shows that the vowel is pronounced with a short sound. (Compare with the entry for **long vowel sound**. Children usually learn the short vowel sounds before the long vowel sounds.)

About the authors and illustrator

Who are the authors?

Elspeth and Rowena are sisters who believe in a world where all children learn to read with confidence *and* have the chance to discover the pleasure of being lost in a good book.

Elspeth is a teacher certified in using the Orton Gillingham approach to teach children with dyslexia and other language-based learning difficulties. She lives with her husband and three children in Vancouver, British Columbia.

Rowena is a children's writer and editor living with her two children in Victoria, British Columbia.

Elspeth

Rowena

Who is the illustrator?

Elisa

Elisa is an award-winning children's book designer, illustrator and author with a passion for language and literacy. Originally from Mexico City, she lives with her husband and two children in Vancouver, British Columbia.

Acknowledgments

We have many people to thank for helping us create this book.

We are grateful to our many "test" readers who commented on early drafts of the stories: Tierra Boorman, Luke Carter, Melissa Carter, Tristan Carter, Daniel Cross, Julia Cross, Janet Elliott, Anne Ellis Clarke, Anna Fong, Meg and Greg Horobin, Miranda Longpre, Leslie O'Hagan, Beverley Rudy, Martine Street, Genevieve Wilson, Madeleine Wilson and numerous students at 44 Sounds Orton Gillingham Learning Studio, at Maria Montessori Academy and in the Richmond School District.

We thank everyone who has shared their expertise with us and helped us launch the *Meg and Greg* books: Jesse Finkelstein, Zoe Grams, Susan Korman, Kate Moore Hermes and Carra Simpson. We are especially grateful to Andrew Wooldridge, Ruth Linka, Liz Kemp and all the other amazing people at Orca Book Publishers who have helped bring Meg and Greg to a wider audience.

Thank you to all the children and their buddy readers who told us how much they enjoyed *Meg and Greg* Book 1 and spurred us on to create Book 2.

And thank you, readers, for joining Meg and Greg on their adventures. We hope you enjoyed reading about their escapades at summer camp as much as we enjoyed creating the stories!

More fun with
Meg and Greg!

Book 1

Book 3

Book 4

"Brings new energy to the
task of learning to read."
—*Kirkus Reviews*